# The Sound
## of the
## Shadow of Her Hands

by

Dan Noyes

ISBN 978-0-359-32443-9

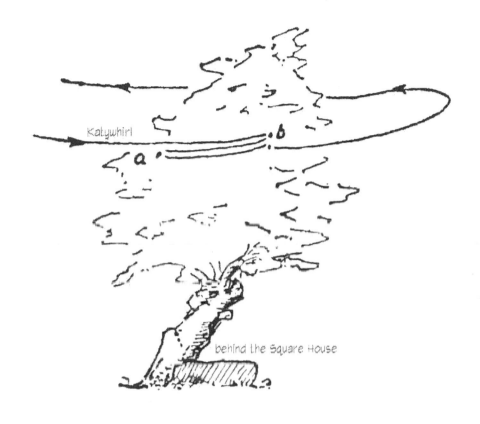

Katywhirl

behind the Square House

## Prelude

The spirit of humanity interconnects us all.
Sometimes it takes a deaf orphan to help us understand
that which is invisible is the most essential.
Through Ulme's journey and observation of life, we are left
to see the back parts of God. Through the silence of
Ulme's world, we start to hear the shadow of her hands.

Gratitude and thanks to my children, Bella, River and Soleil, who embrace poetic living; to my wife, Kerryk, who inspires me and holds my hand as an otter; to Darren Gislason who gave us his enchanted park on the north bank of the Yellow Medicine and to Dana Yost, whose editing comments were from within the story itself.

# Table of Contents

# The Sound of the Shadow of Her Hands

*Since nothing that exists*
*in the world of senses*
*is everlasting,*
*the loss of sense*
*permeates towards eternity.*

## Issuing

It was a quiet night on West Seventh Street and just outside the big white foursquare house lay a somber girl. She was sprawled on the small grass patch just to the side of the front porch. She was trying to get comfortable and escape the heat by making her body contact as much of the cool grass as she could. She could sense the anticipation of dew on the underbelly of each blade of grass. She could hear the pitch of the wind, tuned with the length of each grass stalk as it turned from a high dry rustle and started to move down the scale to a low moan. The summer evening breeze was not only planting the seeds of anticipatory dew but changing its song in the process.

She could not lay flat on her stomach as she wished, but rather stretched the side of her body from arm over head to hip twisted legs. The bulge was also restless tonight, squirming and kicking to the rhythm of the changing wind's song. She missed her parents some, but not enough to write them every day as she had promised. There was too much anger and misunderstanding with her mother and not enough bond with her father. They would see her soon enough as the bulge was ripe and due towards the end of the month. It was August.

As darkness fell over the side yard, she was summoned to bed by someone in the house. She had tried not to know or acknowledge any of them during this time of ripening. They were ethereal to her and she protected the things that lasted. She did the same with the bulge as it was full of guilt and regret and loss. She did turn the sense of loss into another form of feeling. It was compartmentalized in her psyche as a visceral sense. It was beyond what she saw, but it still held a vision. It was palpable. It felt like a pit in her stomach, then took on the faint smell of the tips of walking canes. The rubber tips she smelled in the front closet of her grandparents' house, mixed with the smell of old throw rugs. This smell then shifted to become a strong sweet taste hanging from the sides of her tongue, with a slight burnt caramel that only Mrs. Butterworth's could offer. The sounds were only the kicking of the bulge and its tiny heart beating twice as fast as her own. This all combined to build the sense of loss that she reveled in. This very sense would soon set her free.

Startled by the second call to cajole her inside, she responded, "yes sister, I'll be right there." Issuing could not wait for this endless cycle to be complete and for her sense of loss to win over the monotony.

# Little Ulme

It wasn't easy communicating with people who could listen to anything. They took too much for granted and let every other sound escape their attention. Often, they were too busy making noise to listen. Ulme had just recently realized this. It hadn't become clear for her until she had figured out how to make her own sounds. The click of tongue to teeth and the scoop of discs to roof of mouth were her basics. The world had just grown for her as she realized she could push her legs and pull her hands to scoot around the whitewashed pine floor of the little room she lived in.

Things that had color talked most, although Ulme had
noticed the whispers of the greys and light browns were
most exquisite. She could taste their color as they
murmured their stories of the lonely unforgotten spots.
The rare visits that beings would make when their eyes
would fall upon their space. Ulme liked this best since she
felt appreciated and happy to visit these spaces of color.
The white washed floorboards had several knotholes that
felt like the sound of creased leather. These were the
places she most pondered and wondered and wandered
within. She would often wait for her morning feeding to be
done so she could return to the party on the floor. Other
than her bottle times, she saw no other person. Although
she was still not walking, she had learned to cover her room
from a snail view quite well.

One morning after her feeding she was startled to find
another person, like her, presented to the room. She was
Ulme's size and quite frankly had Ulme's smell, only Ulme
noticed the slight bump of starch wafting from the girl's
gown. With her eyes, she asked the girl's name and why she
looked like the smell of starch, but the girl didn't notice her

question and started to open her mouth while emitting very intense colors of red and yellows. It was as if the newcomer could shoot flowers from her mouth. Her name was Keahps and she quickly established her dominance of Ulme and the room.

This was a time of trying as Ulme no longer had fragrant periods of time to visit her floorboard knots or to observe the taste of the glass windows as they melted. Keahps was always producing colors from her mouth which were so bold and heavy, that they hid the quieter senses of the room. Keahps was able to show Ulme that she could observe things making a vibration without straining to do so. Ulme suddenly realized that they were different. Ulme wondered how such a strange creature had come to her. No one else of her size must be like Keahps.

## For the Birds

Ulme was now at an age of outside. She and Keahps would spend hours in the summer mornings, and again, hours in the summer afternoon playing outside the big white foursquare house. Ulme adored the outside and found pure pleasure in observing everything from the creepy crawlies to the smells of the wind. Ulme tried to share these things with Keahps but Keahps was more interested in projecting the colors from her mouth than taking in something from her senses. Ulme noticed how the grass vibrated a smell of glass when it was short and tasted more to the metallic strings of Mother Superior's cello when the grass had long stalks. It was during that first summer of outside that Ulme fashioned a way to add Keahps' way of looking at the world to her own repertoire of observation. Ulme noticed that Keahps would often turn and look at songbirds, even while projecting colors from her own mouth. Keahps would then change her color projections based on the color of the bird she noticed. Ulme quickly drew together the sense of bird color and Keahps' mouth colors. It was if the bird songs were sculpting the very colors Keahps chose to project from her mouth.

It was some time during this first summer of outside that Ulme realized how valuable Keahps was to her own way of looking at the world. There was something that Keahps was able to take in that Ulme could not. Even though Keahps was loud with her mouth colors, Ulme learned to see past the striking colors to subtler pangs, such as the transition of colors that mimicked the movement of a songbird's beak and staccato of its neck to head twitches. Ulme knew that no one else was like Keahps.

One day as the birds of the afternoon breeze were leaving, Ulme discovered she too could project colors from her mouth if she focused on the birds. The colors come from the birds when they are breathed out and moved their tongue with beak. Ulme fashioned her tongue to mimic a brown cuckoo dove she held with her eyes on the gravel walk at the edge of the treestand. Ulme knew that her tongue could fashion colors with her breath, but she had never been able to articulate which color nor the texture of the color at their edges. But the tongue of the dove was upon the front ridge of her mouth. Ulme could see it as if there was a pocket in the roof of the dove's mouth made just for the tongue to touch. As Ulme moved her own tongue across the roof of her mouth, she felt a similar ridge she could use to connect her tongue and exhale; la. The color conjured from the touch of tongue to dove ridge was yellow with sharp silver tassels of flutter at its edge. As Ulme inhaled, her tongue disengaged from the dove ridge and was drawn atip to the ridge for a yellow second; illa. Involuntarily she let out her little gray slide of breath at the end; ha. Ulme could now speak; la illa ha. She could also see the colors emitting from her mouth as she felt the vibration of birdsmell in her nose.

In the world of sight and taste and touch, sound becomes the anchor to place. It has location and geography as well as its own echolocation of all objects and materials in the surround. Even Ulme knew this because her body could feel sound, except she was limited to audible sounds in the slower vibrations. Because of her sight she knew that bird gathering and singing aligned with sunlight and prosperity. Ulme also knew that she could see these things and Keahps could not.

We are heightened by our imperfections. Only Ulme had no idea her inability to hear bright colors was an imperfection. What she did know was that Keahps could not only hear bright colors but also make them. This reality made Ulme vigilant in her observation of Keahps. In waiting for and watching for bright colors, Ulme was an ever-observant participant in catching the bright colored sounds, even though she could not hear them. And as Keahps and Ulme grew older, Ulme knew that a day would come when they would no longer be together. Keahps would certainly be taken first. This saddened Ulme a wee bit until she quickly circled back to realize she would be left alone with the soft barely speaking colors left in the crooks and crannies of the floorboards. She could return to hearing the lonely colors that could not compete with the brights. Ulme also knew that she could always watch the bright colors speak from the birds that stitch the spirit in us.

Keahps was often oblivious to Ulme in the proceedings of the day, but at times Keahps wanted Ulme's attention, which she could conjure with very little effort. Ulme was the consummate observer of not only Keahps, but of all things. Ulme's ability to perceive was incredibly keen, but her outward expression of perception was as subtle as the lesser perceptions she perceived.

One morning, Keahps was in want. She wanted the attention of Ulme in bearing witness to Keahps. It was past the hour of the early birds but before the morning feeding. Keahps was angry that she was not yet selected and in order to express this she projected loud and vivid hues of orange and blue. Ulme understood the angst within the colors and perceived the general sentiment of the situation. Keahps felt that Ulme needed to give reaction and Ulme's undivided attention was not enough. Without the passing of a moment, Keahps extended her angst to the nightstand by swatting the glass bottle that rested on its outboard half. Ulme watched the extended moment move across the room towards the corner behind the lone chair. As the glass bottle exploded into a myriad of shards that reeked of swollen milk, both Ulme and Keahps jerked with the implosion of the glass that moved in an outward direction within the same fraction of a moment that it recoiled. Both Ulme and Keahps knew that it was a moment of dire consequence. The return of the bottle was needed for the fulfillment of the morning feeding. Not only was the milk precious to the girls but so was the calm delivery of said milk in lieu of stern judgment. Keahps expressed this in lavender as her mouth projected soft discernments that Ulme perceived as some of the kindest auras that Keahps had ever shared with her. Ulme at once knew what to do. She moved with a fluid grace towards the corner behind the unbalanced chair and started to pick up the sharp puzzle pieces with speedy purpose. It took her little time to converse with the matter and to hear how the pieces should speak to one another in order to stack up into the object they once were. She focused her direction in this re-interpretation towards the nightstand and was able to bring about the manifestation of the bottle in short order. There was but one missing piece, but the bottle now stood seemingly intact. The morning sister would surely see the object as whole when entering the room. Ulme quietly spoke to the floorboards to coax them into the parlay of the moment. She interpreted their desire by simply sliding the nightstand an inch over the playful floorboard whose blueish gray crease seesawed by neatlight. For lack of elapsed time, Ulme and Kheaps moved towards the window to anticipate morning feeding by watching the early birds evaporate. Kheaps understood the value of Ulme in the moment and this created a prideful calm in her overall body language. Ulme tasted it in the hushed balmy texture on the surface of the skin of Kheaps. They both knew how the morning feeding would transpire and it brought them closer to one another. One in purpose and the other in pride.

## Not for Keahps

And so, it came to be one bright but cold winter morning, when the floorboards were dryer in their loneliness, and the holy doves were flying from squeaky snow to brittle telephone wire, that Keahps' people came to gather her. Ulme had anticipated this event, although she had no idea how to understand it; how the exchange worked or her own part in the gathering. She had been issued before she could reason and now the plot unfolding before her was re-enacting a new cycle of all that had come to this moment. Keahps was not sad as she glanced over her shoulder and threw one last shout of vibrant scarlet drawn from the holy doves. The ravens where Keahps holy doves and the ravens always spoke in this palette and Keahps always drew from them in the winter times. The gatherers left with Keahps and Ulme was left with the gentle hues. In that moment she saw the floorboard with the gentle blueish gray crease. She dropped to her knees and brought her body into a vertical elliptical ball. Her face was flush against her hands, which cupped the floor. As she communed with the crease, she learned of the cross totter that tick-tocked across the floor with the movement of her breath. She knew that her body was in communing with her room but in that moment, she realized how even her breath conducted the music of the room. The one prodigal shard of glass created seventeen new moons prior was now animated in its beautiful dance across the floor boards. The blueish-gray creased board harmonized with the goat-yellow nail head. The intricate workings of her room reminded Ulme of the pocket watch she once observed being cleaned by the evening watch sister, while waiting for a Keahp's fever to pass. The ebouche plates of the floorboard's translating breath to movement in the pawl of the goat-yellow nail head as the once lost bottle glass shard was brought back into the fold. Its perfected pirouette from one side to another, forward and backward, this way and that, so haphazard yet so perfect. Ulme saw the rhythm of her body's breath in the movement of the shard and the entire room's life enveloped her. Ulme was at one with the world of her room. Her momentary sense of loss for Keahps was replaced with the solemnity of the moment. Her mind resonated with the mechanics of the room and her body. The ribbon she felt could now almost be tasted. It wrapped around her body as it entangled everything around her.

Ulme was at once frantic with delight and paralyzed with the fear of losing the moment. She breathed deeply now. Ulme was realizing the syncopation of her breath frequency at it conversed with the dance of the shard. Ulme noticed the tug of ribbon at the plexus beneath her ribs. This connection to humanity coaxed her to immediate action within the delayed reality of the things. Ulme knew what she must do.

# The Ritual of the Charcoal and the Shard

The lonely objects drew Ulme into compassion and in those moments her mouth naturally uttered la illa ha upon the exhale and il alla hu on the inhale. These words were summoned as her breathing prayer. Rarely were they audible enough for other humans to hear, although there were really no humans to hear. Ulme uttered the sounds for the little things and she knew that they could see her joyous yellow melody with little tinsels of metallic edging. These were the sounds from Ulme's gullet when the universe was conspiring with the little things. It made Ulme happy to know she breathed this prayer in communion with the smallest voices; the voices of the terrazzo doormat and the lumps of charcoal in her drawing bowl and now the milky whisper coming from the bottle shard.

Ulme involuntarily took up the shard and carefully listened to it. She knew it wanted to become part of something more grounded, something more permanent and enduring. The voice of the glass was melting. The voice of the terrazzo was sedimentizing and the moment of the charcoal was right now. Ulme moved the shard in her fingers in order to take note of its fit to her tips. Somehow, she knew that the shard was an instrument of alignment with her body. It had a curvature that made her think of the yearning her pinky felt as it reached for her thumb. And so, she positioned the shard between thumb and pinky finger on her left hand. It created a beautiful arc of reach in which Ulme could foresee the tantalizing motion.

Ulme cherished the taste of her charcoal as it danced in the air. She was only allowed to use it to draw on the cardboard box lids that the sisters gave her on occasion, but she harmonized with that surface as if it were her only friend. The charcoal allowed her to capture the essence of things that could not otherwise be drawn. She could draw the cracked floorboard that teeter-tottered and somehow get it to project colors that she heard the floorboard speak. She could assure this happening as the charcoal dust would land on her tongue mid-flight and allow her sense of taste to conjure the sound of movement. So, it was a sacrifice to use the charcoal beyond its cherished use but Ulme felt compelled to journey into this new ritual.

She had been visiting the travertine for only a short time when an event occurred late one afternoon after feeding. The sister tripped upon the edge of the small frayed rug, just inside the gullet of her little room. After her door was shut and the quiet joy of contemplation was back upon

Ulme, she caught a shimmer and a voice from under the frayed muss at the edge of the up kicked rug. It was this little doormat- sized chunk of frozen earth that had given Ulme such pleasure in the last season. She could have so many conversations deep within the pits and creases of the travertine's personality. There were discussions of the early days of the earth and the flow of lava. There were stories told of being cut from the earth and sown into the wooden floor; regrets and beatifications of glory before and after contact with skin.

That is how Ulme knew she must take the glass shard and the charcoal to the travertine. It was a body's dance that made perfect sense. And so, it went; Ulme caressed the glass shard in her hand with thumb to pinky creating the clear crescent burnisher as a natural extension of her shoulder to elbow out swung and wrist in a palsy stance. The rotation of wrist to brush had become Ulme's own ritual of the ribbon. She would burnish the charcoal into the grooves and stories of the travertine, all while uttering la illa ha upon the exhale and il alla hu on the inhale.

# Beyond the Square House

The days and the rituals within the big square white house were long and cyclical. Ulme grew from one of the floor to one of the chair rail. Looking up gave her a perspective that she knew as her own. Looking up helped her to always be aware of the humble connection she had with all things. At times this hypnotized her as she felt the little muscles in her eyes strain. When this happened, she sat and let the world speak to her in clear tones. Her ability to hear all things was now improving. She could not bring this in through waves of things slapping against each other, but she could witness the slapping and smell the waves. She addressed different smells to different waves and the smell of the door shutting clicked in her nose like the slight tin of tuna with one fleck of pepper announcing the security of latch. It was this way of listening that started to bring her beyond the big white Square House.

In the time of now, Ulme knew she would grow beyond the Square House for the world was coming to her in all of its glory. The universe abounded, and she could hear that more clearly than any sound audible to others. And so, it was time for Ulme to go to the Sister School.

At the age of retaining, the sisters required the children of the Square House to attend the Sister School. Ulme was beyond the age of first retaining, but the sisters did not know that. They simply knew that she could no longer stay in her room all day. The sisters were concerned about the seeming gibberish that they heard Ulme utter. To the sisters, La illa ha il allah hu was not a sign of retaining but they knew they could use repetition and strictness to help Ulme learn to utter at least a few basic words. They had no hopes of civilizing her to a point of adoption, but they did have hopes of getting Ulme to a point of their pride. The Sister School was across the street from the Square House.

Ulme had often caught glimpses of the Sister School. Her bedroom window looked into the back yard, so she could catch a glance when the Square House had to be evacuated for the monthly fire drill or during the summer outdoor time. This is when Ulme was able to escape the Square House through its back stairs and rear door. The Sister School could be seen through the scant angle between the backyard and the linen shop next door. Ulme could see two windows of the Sister School and three times she even saw children behind the windows. This was always during a fire drill when the children were not attending the Sister School as it was the summer outdoor time. Ulme's joy was not hampered by restriction; she saw and felt only the expanse of all things before her and of this mindset, she knew the Sister School.


## The Sister School

'La illa ha il allah hu' was so much easier to breath than the new prayer the sisters imposed upon Ulme, 'Lord Jesus Christ, Son of God, have mercy on me, a sinner.' Ulme knew that the prayers were the same, but the new version felt awkward to her mouth, tongue and ears. It was not filled with the same warmth and love of the proclamation that 'all is God.'
The sisters were eager to help Ulme understand the meaning of the last word of the Jesus prayer for it came with pain, which Ulme had to also learn. Ulme had always felt any touch sensation as love but now she was made to understand that some touch sensations were meant to be displeasurable. This came in the form of wooden rulers, beautiful wooden rulers. Ulme made sure to never

intermingle the beauty of the ruler with the sensation that was intended as pain, and thus she learned sin.

But she adapted and learned to add color to the Jesus prayer to take away the sinner. She could do this with just a scent of lavender brushed over the top of the ending of the word. The sisters simply thought her messy utterances were tangled with French accents for some reason. Ulme knew that changing the red of the word sinner to a lavender crescendo would erase pain, for it tapped into some foreign verbal beatification that she could not yet understand, nor could anyone. In her room at night, Ulme always returned to La illa ha il allah hu as it harmonized with her breathing so much better. Only now, Ulme had combined the lavender accent to 'all is God.' The curving and cupping of her tongue would scoop the lavender discs and make any word end in light.

And so Ulme began to understand how to combine things to create a richer experience. The once-alarming and awkward prayer had become a crease of light and that same discovery of light because of its awkwardness, had now shed itself upon her beloved prayer.

22

# Journey to the Gaps

Ulme was alone by most normal standards, only she did not know this. The Sisters had stopped trying to teach her after they were successful in getting Ulme to recite the Jesus prayer, for they felt her salvation was secure with her capable of that prayer. And so Ulme started to be left alone and even avoided in the Sister School. Ulme went further into her connection with the ribbon that connects us all; for it is unseen and thus the most essential. It was also the ribbon that kept her world together for her first several years within her room. She had learned to fester the ribbon by remaining open to experiences of the extreme, as was the case with Kheaps. And then, to return to the ribbon of the unseen when it was only Ulme. This allowed Ulme to converse with the universe of the floorboards as wells as the flight and song of the birds. Ulme called this, in her own mind, the world of the gaps. The places between things. The places where no one else cared to look or speak.

The moments of the days of the years passed while Ulme discovered more and more of the gaps. Her world had become robust within the gaps. It was as if the smallest moment of dust could be observed to play out a universe of excitement and joy. It was within one of these moments of dust that Ulme recalled her mother.

It was a quiet sunny afternoon in Ulme's room. It was of the cold months, and during these months, in the late afternoon sun, Ulme could best visit with the dust. Her room had one window that served to usher in the sunlight when the shadows become longer. The angle of these sun-setting rays seemed to lift the dust in jubilation over the warmth it ensued. Ulme had learned that the warmth of the rays hitting her floorboards would inflate specks of dust into vessels of sun-swollen air. These moments she named Vance as they progressed the quiet specks into rapturous epiphones of dance. It was this afternoon that Ulme noticed Vance afloat and in mid-gyration when a sub-speck of other was issued forth, and one Vance became two. It immediately brought her to the deeply buried memory of being issued herself. She knew not from what mother Vance she was issued, but from one swollen speck she knew she was ushered and had become the other of the one. This, at the age of twelve sets of seasons, became the knowledge for Ulme and awareness of Issuing. And though she had never again met her mother following birth, she knew of her in act and in observation of the specs of dust she called Vance.

## Issuing Returns

Ulme did not have someone to talk to or to ask about the feelings of her mother nor did she realize this was an option: to talk to and confide in another human being. But she did learn to confide in the colors she heard.

At first Ulme didn't understand the lack of her ability to hear but she did perceive how others around her seemed to react to the breezes within their ears. Ulme felt the movement of air within her ears as well but she could not articulate them into her mind as she witnessed others do. The sisters often would turn to react to something they had not seen when Ulme felt the movement of air within her ears. Ulme was able to understand that what others felt was sound where she saw colors.

In just that previous spring, Ulme had watched closely over the moon of the green grass as her favorite cluster of grain sheaf grass grew around her beloved gnarly oak tree. She watched this grass from her window for the entire lunar cycle. Ulme noticed that the grass on the west side of the great tree grew the fastest and the tallest and she could hear why. The larkspur-blue mist that the grasses danced with the wind were making them stronger. The mid-range dancing color was around 670 clicks at a time where the grasses on the leeward side of the great oak spoke in orange to yellow dance in a slow waltz with the wind. The low-range dancing waltz of some 490 clicks at a time did not temper the stalks of grass as vigorously as those on the west speaking larkspur. In this observation leading into the moon of the green leaves, Ulme was able to test her observation again and the leaves accomplished their dance with much more obvious results for the entire great oak was much more developed and robust on the west side. Here the tree received both much-needed sunlight and the proper symbiotic dance with the wind to make it strong and thus grow faster and larger. In these two cycles of the moon, Ulme fashioned her belief that her own vibrations must be held high. The more clicks she could dance with around her being; the more she would grow and understand her communion with the world around her through the universe and with God. This brought Ulme back to an even

stronger belief in and desire to live within her breath prayer;
La illa ha il allah hu.

Ulme now understood that the colors she witnessed in all
things were their vibrations. She knew that all things had
spirit that held them together and in this understanding of
spirit-holding matter, Ulme began to interpret a new
language. She could see the vibrant lavender emitting from
a bumble bee flying past her window. She could then see
the lavender for what it was. In now her thirteen sets of
seasons, Ulme began to understand that the lavender
perceived in the color was the vibration ushered forth from
the spirit of the bumble bee and Ulme could start to hear
the vibrations in the 700 clicks per second range.

And in the moon of ripeness of her thirteenth set of
seasons, Ulme heard a voice. She was at first in disbelief.
The movement of air hit her ear and swooshed straight
through to her brain. She didn't understand where it came
from, but she did hear the words clearly; "oh, she is deaf."
This event happened one late afternoon when the sisters
where all but done putting the girls through the motions of
the day within the classroom. The mother sister was at the
open door of the classroom and a woman was standing
behind her. The woman wore clothes unlike the sisters and

Ulme knew she was from beyond the Sister School. As soon as the disbelief of hearing settled her senses, Ulme looked to the door and felt the glance of the woman fall upon her. The woman spoke no more or at least Ulme could not perceive hearing as she just had a moment before. The glance of the woman fell upon Ulme with slow clicks and the color of deep red. Ulme had never seen such a slow- clicking red before. She knew if something clicked so slow, it was either very unhealthy or very unhappy. The woman turned and walked away and Ulme was left to translate the first words her ears had ever delivered to her mind. The entire event over several moments left Ulme confused and somewhat dazed. Her own vibrations had just been moving fast but now they slowed to match those of the red she saw in the glance of the woman. Ulme suddenly knew the woman was the one who had issued her into this world. Ulme also felt she would never see the woman again.

Throughout that night Ulme found herself seeing many slow vibrations of color. The world around her was tinted with a scarlet hue. It was thick and so slow- moving that Ulme felt she was beneath the water and struggled to breath. Only after gasping several times in her sleep, only to awaken herself; Ulme realized the slow-vibrating hues were coming from herself and mixing with the vibrations around her to slow everything down. Ulme went to her breath prayer to hasten her own vibrations as she fell back to sleep, and in doing so, she awoke to her room alive and vibrating at a beautifully high chant. Her beloved charcoal and shard were singing to the floorboards and the crevasses within the floorboards were alive with a bazaar of activity. Ulme had her answer. She knew from where she was issued and she knew that all would be fine in the world. It was time for Ulme to move out and beyond the limitations of the Square House and the Sister School. Ulme was free.

## The Holy Dove

Ulme was fond of mourning doves as their song was so happy and comforting. There was one dove that Ulme had known for many seasons. Ulme called this dove, Holy, for the dove's coo could be seen by Ulme as a radiant violet that vibrated at such a high rate that it set Ulme's own vibration to that of the Holy.

In her observation, Ulme knew that Holy was from beyond the Square House. She knew that Holy simply visited the Square House alley wires in the morning. Holy knew that the sun was perfectly aligned with her daily perch and the scattered leftover rice that spilled from the Square House trash stroller. Ulme herself had taken out the trash stroller from nightly bussing duty she had held for over five sets of seasons. This was the same amount of time she had known Holy.

Ulme saw Holy fly away each morning in the same direction, towards the West, into the morning breeze. Ulme also noticed that Holy landed on the alley wire from the same direction; that of the Thunderbeings and the weather. This is how Ulme aligned with the idea of heading to the west and migrating her life from beyond the Square House and Sister School to the city about her small universe, and even beyond that.

Holy had given Ulme the courage and belief that she could reach beyond what she knew, for Ulme had never been beyond the Square House or the Sister School. The homing nature of Holy gave Ulme confidence in an ability to find her way back home; to a home she had never been to before. It was this letting go of fear and trusting in the unknown that set Ulme further free and in her breathing prayer she confided, La illa ha il allah hu.

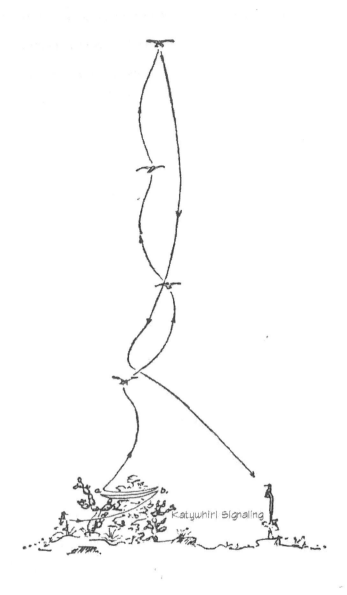

Katywhirl Signaling

## Katywhirl

Holy had given Ulme the courage, but it was another bird,
dazzling and vibrating that instilled the instinct to survive on

32

her own. The Moon of the Ripeness brought this high-vibrating bird to Ulme's world. The bird moved so quickly and with such hushed himmelblau whirls that it took many visits before Ulme could catch the bird in still sight and make a non-vibratory connection. The bird's name was Katywhirl, after the glorious green insects that chirped the same vibrations as the Katywhirl's wings in flight.

Katywhirl also fascinated Ulme in its attraction to the lower vibrating colors. Katywhirl was drawn to the scarlets and reds that Ulme heard in her memories of Issuing. But Katywhirl was able to transform the somber unhappiness of the scarlet into a vibrant, lavender, vaporous color that sprinkled itself as a top note over the hushed himmelblau whirls of Katywhirl's flying dance. This transformation from slow somber clicks of color into higher vibrating colors was akin to Ulme's use of color in transforming the Jesus Prayer from pain to joy in the sprinkling of lavender over its ending crescendo. The vibration of color had become Ulme's ultimate sense of being in the universe. Her understanding of the interconnectedness and interactional result of all vibrations had helped her to take confidence in moving without fear, beyond the only universe she had known. Ulme was free from Issuing and this freedom had allowed her to manifest her understanding and union with her surroundings as a calm and embracing love. Ulme had no idea what lay ahead of her and that unknowing is what left her breathing, La illa ha il allah hu.

Katywhirl visited Ulme in the afternoons that midsummer. In the poppyreds growing at the back of the Square House yard Katywhirl vibrated and whirled her glory. It was upon her seventeenth connection with Ulme, that Katywhirl understood the vibration she was tasting within the poppyreds. The vibrations were being altered by Ulme's breathing prayer and Katywhirl embraced the connection. Katywhirl hovered, whirled and danced in both an embracing movement as a whole and vibration as a being of which Ulme knew to take special note. Katywhirl had decided to show Ulme how to harvest vibration and nourishment from the flowers. The very nectar that Katywhirl lapped up with ravenous zeal could also be ingested with the vessel that held the nectar. Katywhirl tore a tiny zucchini blossom from the poppyreds and hovered above Ulme's philtrum and slid the tiny blossom down the crevasse slide. Ulme savored and finally chewed with delight as the vibration of the blossom and its stewed release to the nectar started to vitalize her. Ulme now knew she could sustain herself. With the help of two birds and

her breathing prayer, she had gained enough courage to
follow Katywhirl towards the Thunderbeings. It was the
first of many steps that would bring her to her before-home.
The one she had never seen but had known.

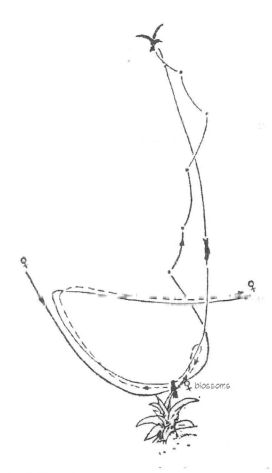

blossoms

## Towards the Thunderbeings

Ulme left the Square House in the midst of the cricket and
katydid chirps. She wore her Sister School uniform; a
butter yellow jumper with CSJ embroidered over her heart.

Ulme carried nothing with her other than a bag of pecans she had saved from the previous winter celebration. She knew her subsistence relied upon Katywhirl's guidance and that is who she followed from the backyard of the Square House. It was mid-afternoon, and no one noticed her walking away. Ulme kept a mindful feel of Katywhirl's vibrations and stopped to ingest all of the same flower vessels of nectar that Katywhirl led her to. She walked west until past dusk and nestled into the brush below Katywhirl hanging in her own torpor.

Katywhirl had shown her how to slow her vibrations to a deep and relaxed breathing; guided by her breathing prayer, La illa ha il allah hu. Ulme felt connected to the universe and to her friend, who hung a few feet above her.

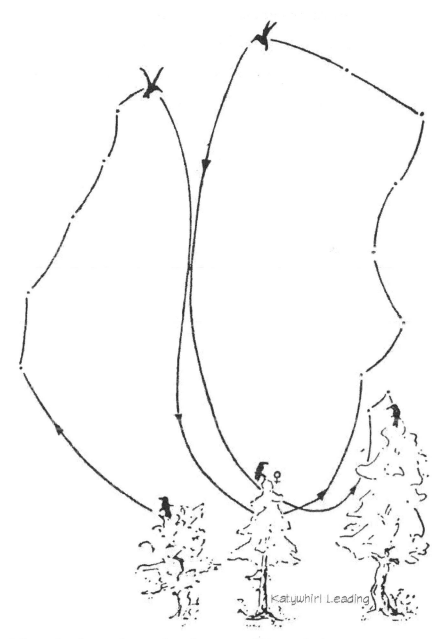

Katywhirl Leading

Ulme slowly awoke to the chirping of Katywhirl's wings.
Ulme rubbed her eyes and saw that Katywhirl was already
feeding on some nearby blossoms. Ulme followed suit and

after eleven blossoms were sipped and eaten, the two of them were off towards the west once again.

It took two full days after that first morning to reach a place that felt beyond the congestion of the city. Ulme felt no fatigue nor hunger as the vibration and routine the girl and bird had devised was enlightening. Ulme was able to pick up upon so many new vibrations, sights and colors. She had never been beyond the the Sister School and the Square House, thus the universe was full of wonderment and joy. Ulme had never felt so alive and connected to everything about her. This began the moon of ripeness. The cricket and katydid chirps were in full blossom and their colors kept Ulme company.

Ulme began to take account of the terrain she was walking daily and soon began to notice that there was always the vibration of water flowing in the near distance. She trusted Katywhirl and knew that the path towards the Thunderbeings was also routed where the water scraped across the land and flowed back towards the city. Ulme was journeying against this flow and it registered a deep inner understanding of her path towards origin; her own origin.

This journey with Katywhirl had become Ulme's life. It was as if the journey was becoming the place she yearned for. The ritual of Katywhirl's chirping wings waking Ulme to the first rays of sun and the constant reflection upon the dazzling flower colors and sounds that she would sip and chew, had become not the journey, but the destination itself. Ulme now understood Katywhirl's flight patterns and heard them in the colors of Katywhirl's vibrations.

## The Restoration of Vibration

Ulme noticed time passing as the butter-yellow vibration of her jumper had slowed to some 577 clicks per second. Her journey had not only affected the color but the CSJ embroidered over her heart had lost several of its stitches. Ulme had grown accustomed to rubbing the CSJ at night upon falling to sleep with her breathing prayer. She now counted seventeen loose threads as she stroked the CSJ with her glass shard ritual finger. She wanted to remember everything about her seasons in the Square House and her room. She missed the ritual of the charcoal and the glass shard and thus she picked up a smooth pebble that fit into her hand with the same movement as the glass shard. The stone fit between her thumb and pinky with slight indentations to grip. Although the pebble was smooth, it had a delicate edge to it on the outboard side. As Ulme gripped the pebble, she thought of how the size of a pebble is right now. The intimacy with this old kin brought her comfort and she felt the connection of the universe to the pebble, to Katywhirl and to the glass shard she had left behind. Ulme suddenly thought to coax Katywhirl towards the sound of the flowing water.

## Praying with Otter

Katywhirl was happy to oblige following Ulme towards the big flowing water, although until now, they had only stopped to drink from the smaller streams leading towards the larger. Katywhirl had shown Ulme how clear and sweet the water was at the source. Whenever they had stopped to drink, they had followed the little streams away from the big flowing water until it became tiny. There they would drink.

Ulme wanted deeper water so she could bathe and create a new ritual of scraping her jumper with the smooth pebble she now called Ella.

As Katywhirl first and Ulme with Ella second approached the big flowing water, Katywhirl flew and vibrated a swoop dance out above the water and then back into a small pool. Ulme saw that it was another small stream entering into the big flowing water. Ulme suddenly realized how all waters were connected and held their vibrations as one. This made Ulme happy, as the sun shone down upon her and her friends. Katywhirl landed on a small blade of grass with a hanging belly of dew drop. As Katywhirl landed, she looked to the edge of the pond, which directed Ulme's glance to an incredible vibration. Right where the connected water embraced the grassy edge was a muddy slide and in the middle of the slide was a furry creature that Ulme knew to be called an Otter.

Ulme and Ella gently made their way towards the pond. Ulme entered the soft mushy edge of the pond to stand waist deep in the connected water. She stood still for moments so she could feel the vibrations of the Otter, which now lie on his back at the end of the slide. Ulme was confused for some time as the vibrations she felt from the

Otter where not consistent with its color. She had expected clicks in the 650 per second range but the Otter was vibrating well above 700 clicks per second. Ulme had never experienced vibrations that had not aligned with the colors she knew. Ulme understood that something extraordinary was about to happen.

Some 500 seconds had elapsed since Ulme had entered the pond and although everything was vibrating, it was also still. Ulme, without thinking, held Ella in her hand, between thumb and pinky. She extended her reach towards the Otter and as Ulme moved, the Otter reached into a small fold of skin under his left arm. He sat up slightly and pulled out his own Ella, which he extended towards Ulme. The Otter then slid into the pool and both Otter, Ulme and their two Ellas began to splash and play. The universe was alive with vibration and connection. Ulme realized that the Otter had been praying his own breathing prayer upon seeing her. He had raised his vibrations beyond his color. Ulme understood this and immediately understood the connection of prayer and the vibrations of the universe.

Ulme, the Otter and their two Ellas continued to splash and swim around each other with delight and admiration.

Ulme started to use her Ella to scrape and work the color of her jumper back to higher vibrations. The Otter used his Ella to preen his fur. The two harmonies of vibration settled into one cacophony until Ulme felt clean and refreshed. The Otter and Ulme exchanged Ellas and with Katywhirl's lead, they parted ways.

Katywhirl quickly led Ulme and Ella back to the path along the far bank of the big flowing water. Here the red cedar trees gave way to pastures and the walking was effortless. The open air also gave Ulme and Ella a better sense of the beautiful sky dance that Katywhirl vibrated as she led the three further west.

Ulme, Katywhirl and now Ella, had followed the big flowing water from its far North bank the entire journey. Ulme had always felt the vibration of the water's flow beneath her and to the south. One day Katywhirl led Ulme and Ella to the shores of the big flowing water. Katywhirl did this with incredible acrobatic antics that produced such a vibration that Ulme and Ella knew to follow. Katywhirl was on the south side of the big flowing water, where a small stream entered it. Ulme noticed the sand bar created by the joining of the two waters and, with Ella in hand, she waded slowly through the big flowing water. Ulme was walking on the mushy floor of the big flowing water beyond the height of her waist. She held Ella above her and followed Ella outreached as a guide. Ulme felt the vibration and flow of the water and allowed herself to be connected with it by balancing herself with her feet yet letting go of her body as the flow surrounded her. Once the water had reached the CSJ embroidered over her heart, she felt the mushy floor turn to sand. Ulme started to rise from the water with Ella and soon they were on the south bank of the big flowing water.

Ulme was wet but felt warmed by the sun as it sat high in the sky. Before Ulme could dry off, Katywhirl continued to dance her flight with the same height of vibration as she had before Ulme and Ella entered the water. Ulme realized she needed to get to the North side of the little stream she had just encountered. The north bank of the little stream was covered with delicate yellow flowers. As Ulme and Ella crossed the little stream, water only reached Ulme's knees. As Ulme held Ella outreached, she grabbed for the delicate yellow flower nearest her on the north bank and pulled herself to land. Ulme held her hand out upon losing her grip on the flower stem and found her hands full of dried seeds from the plant that were as crescent moons. Ulme was in amazement at the vibration of the flower seeds and placed them in her jumper pocket. Ulme became aware of the abundance of these flowers along the north bank of the little stream. She knew Katywhirl would be following their path as the little stream flowed back against their journey.


## Pajutazee

Before the journey could get fully back into its cadence, Katywhirl, Ulme and Ella saw a movement in the little stream's bank. The movement was full of vibration and, as Ulme approached, Katywhirl circled. A small Boy emerged from the Moonseed plants and froze in front of Ulme and Ella.

The Boy was browner than Ulme, but like the Otter, he too vibrated at a pace beyond his color. The boy was not speaking but rather emitting a rhythmic gasp of utterances- wóchekiye mitakuye oyasin hau. The Boy repeated this under his breath until Ulme could confidently repeat the same utterance under her own breath. After the Boy and Ulme had started to coincide the harmony of their utterances, Ulme understood this to be the Boy's own breathing prayer and she immediately felt one with the Boy.

Ulme slowly approached the Boy she now knew as Wóche. She held her hand outstretched with Ella grasped between her forefinger and pinky. Wóche reached for his right ear and, with one movement, he removed his own Ella from a tether on his ear. The two children exchanged Ellas without hesitation and Wóche turned into the vegetation and was gone. So much vibration was occuring in such a small place of time that Ulme was not certain if minutes or hours had elapsed. She gently held her new Ella between her forefinger and pinky to find it fit even better than the Ella before or the Ella before that. Ulme felt the universe in harmony and was thankful for her new Ella and her new friend, Wóche. It was time to return to her journey along the new path, flanking the north side of the little stream, amidst the moonseed plants.

Ulme had noticed the chipmunks looking back towards the Thunderbeings for days now. The evenings had grown brisk and Ulme for the first time was feeling her own vibrations slow. She was cold and could not warm herself no matter how she tried. Ulme could feel the universe changing. Although all growing things were becoming ripe, they were also beginning to bow and wilt. Summer was all but over and Ulme knew that her journey needed to culminate with a place she could find warmth. Ulme had felt no fear or sadness in her journey. Hunger was kept at bay by Katywhirl's direction to soft and sweet vessels of blossoms, filled with nectar stew. But the blossoms had become harder to find over the last few days, when, finally one morning, Ulme awoke to find Katywhirl no longer waiting for her. Ulme understood that her friend needed to move towards the sun to stay warm. Ulme also realized that Katywhirl would not leave her unless it was meant to be. Ulme took this to be the universe leading her to a shift in her journey.

## The Boxelder Bug and the Everyday Poet

Ulme and Ella were at the edge of a large stand of trees that crowded the north bank of the little stream that Ulme had now begun to call the Yellow Moon Stream. She felt its vibrations near that of yellow and the moonseed plants growing all along its course had etched their radicles into Ulme's vibration vision.

In this first morning of feeling the absence of Katywhirl, Ulme was keen to pick up on other, higher vibrations. Ulme did not have to walk far before she entered the large stand of trees. Ulme wondered why the underbrush was gone and there was nothing to delay or challenge her gait, but the small flower beds etched across the little forest. Ulme had not seen such an abundance of flowers and food for days. She stopped and began to sip and chew any of the flowers she felt sustenance vibrating from.

Ulme walked from flower bed to flower bed, sipping and chewing until she felt completely ready to take a moment to wonder beyond her stomach. At the moment this wonder ensued, Ulme caught sight of a little green and red house built up in one of the trees. Ulme could feel the vibration from within the house and, even from afar, she understood the vibration of the tree was in harmony with the wind, as well as with the inhabitant within, who she could not see.

That is probably the moment I looked out the window and peered across the speck of a girl, in a faded yellow overall, peering back at me. I decided it best to sit still and concentrate on my breathing, while reciting my most recent poetic find. It was a haiku from Persia; quite possibly by a disciple of Rumi's.

*Only Breath Between*
*Parts the Air and Circles Back*
*Making All things Whole*

Upon my seventeenth recitation of my Breath Poem, the little speck of yellow had turned into a young girl with an outreached arm. Just one arm, outreached. It took until my 21st recitation that I could focus on the small pebble she was holding out towards me. I had never seen such a sight, yet I knew it: Jamais Vu. It was such a lovely and poetic image that I didn't know what to do. I could tell that the girl also was repeating some sort of incantation as her lips were slightly moving with the same calligraphic repetition, I absorbed but did not readily realize. It was as if my senses had crossed and I was hearing things I saw and seeing things I felt. All I could do, after a considerable time of minute movement, was to reach for my table of pebbles and fumble over which was the best to offer her. I only collected schist at that time; little red and rounded off loaves of schist. I grabbed a piece of red schist which was rounded on all but one little odd edge. I knew this was not aligned with her pebble, but it was what I had to offer.

I descended the quick three board steps from treehouse to ground and stood before the girl. She was darker-skinned than most around here and her eyes held saucers of the universe. She was barefooted and, although not tidy, she was clean and groomed. I would have thought her a wild-child if not for her yellow overalls with CSJ embroidered over her heart. We simultaneously exchanged pebbles and I marveled as she placed her new pebble, with one intentional movement, between her left forefinger and pinky.

I took the pebble she had given me and fumbled to place it between my fingers, as she had done. I dropped the stone and we both giggled under our breaths. I dropped the stone a second time and we both laughed aloud. I finally got the stone to rest comfortably between my left forefinger and pinky at which time she crouched down to the earthen floor and wrote the word Ulme in the foot-tamped loam. The girl then uttered the word Ulme. She went back to writing the word Ella and pointed to her new stone and to mine.

The spirit of the girl rang at a high pitch, yet she was calm. She was as the river next to us: flowing with no forcing or holding back. I had to learn more about her as the two of us stood in silence, communicating only through our breathing. Suddenly I thought to lead her into the tree house, where I had a box full of crayons and craft paper. She calmly followed me and understood what I had laid out for her, yet she took a small dry twig and held it to the candle I always kept burning while present in the tree house. I was amazed at what she did next.

Ulme took the charred end of the twig and began to draw a house with a tree and a bird. At first the images were quite child-like and broad-sweeping in their line work, but she began to refine them with the sharp edge of her Ella. At once pushing the charcoal dirt from one pile to the next and erasing some of the dirt in the process. Soon I saw a beautiful scene of a large four-square house with a tree behind it and a small bird flying with an acrobatic movement of faint charcoal which immediately appeared as the bird's flight patterns.

Sheet after sheet of brown craft paper she filled with dirt and sculpted with Ella until I knew her entire story. It suddenly struck me that now with her fourth Ella in hand, she had nowhere to go. It was me as her guide or her home or both. Fear struck me for a moment as I was a middle-aged single man, living a simple life; a bit in town and as much as I could in my beloved park. But that feeling passed as quickly as it came as the energy that Ulme emitted was both calming connection and spirited inspiration.

We spent the remainder of the afternoon with the girl drawing and me interpreting. It was now the long hour, when the sun's shadow extends beyond the height of things it gazes upon. I was getting hungry and wanted to head back to town.

Ulme understood and motioned that she would stay put as she descended the three board steps and walked to the nearest flower bed. She plucked several blossoms, and with grace and wonderment, she sipped the blossoms first and then nibbled them down. Dumbstruck and bewildered, I walked to the edge of the park and drove my old beater down the two-path grassy, onto the county road and back to town.

At home I was elated to find my cousin and house-mate Bill. I quickly explained the experience in meeting Ulme and Ella. Bill seemed not struck by the idea, but rather calm and expecting. We made some sandwiches, Bill grabbed his clavichord and we made our way back to my park. It was dusk.

Bill seemed calmly possessed as we drove the five-mile trek. He said very little but smiled with his big rosy cheeks and nodded at my exclamations. We stopped the car at the park's edge. Bill had his clavichord under arm and we both walked an eager line to the tree house.

There was no Ulme to be found, but rather than look for her or utter her name, Bill took the lead and climbed the three board steps up and into the tree house. I lit the candle and Bill sat before his clavichord and began to play one of his favorite Bach compositions. I had always wondered about Bill's clavichord, as it played so softly. One could barely hear it unless one rested your hand on its wooden chamber cover. I knew from watching Bill play in similar fashion fefore, that he was coaxing the boxelders to join us. It was the month for the silent friends to be about us and as expected one came out to join our vigil gathering. As the triumphant little bug climbed aboard the clavichord, Ulme appeared from the shadows of the candle light. She stood below the tree house and was humming the Bach song along with Bill's finger dance and the boxelder bugs swaying. Bill quietly uttered something under his breath, in a voice that barely vibrated the air to carry. I understood it after contemplating it for a few moments. He had said, "she is deaf." As it registered, I stopped to think about it. It had not registered with me before, but I shuffled through the twenty-some pictures that Ulme had sculpted earlier. By candle light I held one up and saw a new meaning in the scene. It was a depiction of Ulme with several other girls, standing as if in a chorus, with a woman in a habit playing the piano. I had not caught the detail earlier, when Ulme was sculpting it, but now I saw Ulme's hand in the picture resting atop the piano with light vibration lines emitting from her hand.

Ulme climbed the three steps to join us and, although I introduced her to Bill, they both calmly acted as if they knew each other. At the conclusion of the Bach concerto, Ulme clapped and began to speak aloud to us, "La illa ha il allah hu." After she said this several times, we understood that it was as natural as her breath itself. Both Bill and I began to recite the syllables and after all three of us began to breath and utter in unison, Ulme startled us by proclaiming; "All is Gooood." This was the first time I heard the inflection in her voice that gave her deaf voice away. Ulme and I had communicated all day without her uttering but a few syllables.

Bill, as if spoken to directly by God, solemnly stated, "we must walk with Ulme to the Blies." This made sense to me. All of the feelings and reflections that I had experienced throughout the day, in meeting Ulme, and up to this moment, were pure poetry. I felt as if I was living a poem and who best to direct this poetic life but the Blies. So, with the night filled with poetic promise, Ulme and I grabbed our Ellas and Bill swooped his clavichord under his arm and we were off. This would start us on a 20-odd-mile journey by ditch path and creek hollow to the northwest.

And so, the two Everyday Poets walked on either side of Ulme. Ulme held her Ella with slight outreach, as did I. The moon was full and lit our way through the knee-high grasses. All three of us held our vibrations high as we breathed our walking prayers and admired the night.

1. The Square House and Sister School
2. Otter
3. Boy
4. the Tree House
5. the Blies

## Postlude

The journey itself is a revelry in the moment and the moment is now. Ulme, unbeknownst to those around her, lives a poetic life. One filled with wonderment and awe at all the lesser things heralded as equals amidst the grandeur. Her life and journey are fulfilled in the moment of her breathing prayer as well as her ritual of the charcoal and the shard.

Ulme's desire to find and know her mother is fulfilled in the understanding of her connectedness with all things. Thus, Ulme could accept and feel whole even in the rejection from her mother. The journey is fulfilled in jumping into the poetic life; no forcing and no holding back. Like a river which led Ulme and Katywhirl and the reflections in the moment exemplified by Ella, Ulme flows whole. Her family is the everyday poets and her home is with them as well as with the particles of dust.

Reference of Katywhirl Flight Patterns
From *A Study of Bird Song* by Edward A. Armstrong, Dover Publications, New York, 1963.

Cover Image by Angelica Sedano

Dan Noyes was raised on a farm in Southwestern Minnesota, near Ghent. Dan's parents, Ray and Colleen, adopted him as a baby and provided him an enchanted boyhood, filled with wonder. He has been an art, design and architecture professor for years. He practices architecture with Sperides Reiners Architects, where he has great mentors and tries to be one as well. He has a small design studio where he sculpts "spirit holding matter," and teaches autistic students to sculpt, while they help Dan see wider and wilder.

Made in the USA
Middletown, DE
18 February 2019